AFFILIATE MARKETING FOR BEGINNERS

The Definitive Guide to Avoiding Deadly Affiliate Marketing Mistakes

CLARA JOSEPH

All rights reserved. No part of this publication may be reproduced, distributed or transmitted in any form without the permission of the publisher, except as permitted by copyright law.

Copyright © Clara Joseph, 2024.

Introduction

Chapter 1

Understanding the Basics of Affiliate Marketing
    Profit Potential and Difficulties of Affiliate Marketing
        Profit Potential
        Difficulties

Chapter 2

The Evolution of Affiliate Marketing

Chapter 3

Choice of Product or Niche

Chapter 4

Failing to Build a Solid Foundation

Chapter 5

Ignoring Legal and Compliance Issues in Affiliate Marketing

Chapter 6

SEO Monitoring and Traffic Generation

Chapter 7

Poorly Executed Campaigns and Advertising
    The Value of Skillfully Designed Advertisements and Campaigns
    Drawbacks of Badly Done Advertisements and Campaigns

Techniques for Developing Successful Campaigns
How to Recognise the Demands of Your Audience and Steer Clear of Spam Tactics

Chapter 8

Neglecting to Develop Relationships

Chapter 9

Lack of Tracking and Analytics

Chapter 10

People Harmed By Dubious Affiliate Schemes
Dangers Connected with Dubious Affiliate Schemes
How To Determine Trustworthy Affiliate Networks
Warning Signs to be Aware of in Affiliate Marketing
How to Keep Your Brand Integrity and Reputation Intact

Chapter 11

Prevent Burnout and Foster Long-Term Success
Managing Expectations in Affiliate Marketing
Avoiding Burnouts and Maintaining Balance
Long-Term Plans for Sustainable Success

Conclusion

Introduction

In the dynamic realm of digital commerce, affiliate marketing is a source of opportunity, which offers individuals the promise of financial freedom and business success.

However, among the fascination of passive income and lucrative brand partnerships, lie difficulties that can derail even the most promising affiliate businesses.

Welcome to "Affiliate Marketing for Beginners: The Definitive Guide to Avoiding Deadly Mistakes in Affiliate Marketing". In this comprehensive guide, we will begin our journey to reveal the serious mistakes and difficulties that can lead to disaster for affiliate marketers.

From affiliates who are just starting out and looking to advance into the digital landscape to skilled marketers looking to refine their strategies, this guide is a must-have resource for everyone.

We will be examining the complex mechanics of affiliate marketing, study its fundamentals, and explore the complexities behind how it works. We illuminate the commission structures, cookie tracking, and attribution models, providing affiliates with the knowledge to steer the affiliate landscape with confidence and precision. But our journey goes beyond simple techniques.

We will highlight the ethical considerations and compliance standards that govern affiliate marketing, while emphasizing the importance of transparency, integrity and trust to foster long-term relationships along with the audience and the brand.

Getting insights from industry experts, real-life case studies, and first-hand experience. This book provides readers with practical strategies for avoiding difficulties often encountered and charting the path to long-term success in affiliate marketing.

Whether it's avoiding the difficulties of market saturation, mastering the art of traffic generation, or cultivating a resilient mindset in the face of adversity, this guide offers invaluable advice to help affiliates steer the turbulent waters of digital marketing.

As we embark on this journey together, let us arm ourselves with knowledge, foresight, and an unwavering commitment to excellence. With this book as our compass, we are ready to take on the challenge, seize the opportunity, and chart the path towards mastering the art of affiliate marketing.

Join us in bringing to light the mysteries, revealing the truth, and empowering ourselves to overcome the fatal flaws that threaten to sabotage our success.

Together, let's embark on a transformative journey to master and thrive in the ever-changing world of affiliate marketing.

Chapter 1

Understanding the Basics of Affiliate Marketing

Affiliate marketing works on a performance-based model, a dynamic strategy in which companies, often called advertisers or merchants, form a relationship with affiliates, who are called marketers or publishers.

These affiliates play a vital role in promoting the merchant's products or services to their respective audiences, using various marketing channels to generate specific actions such as leads, clicks or sales.

In exchange for their promotional efforts, affiliates are rewarded with a predetermined commission or compensation for each successful referral or conversion they facilitate. This compensation model is directly linked to affiliate performance, ensuring that they are propelled to produce tangible results.

One of the biggest strengths of affiliate marketing is the ability to leverage the influence and reach of the affiliate. These individuals or organizations often have their own audiences or established platforms, from websites and blogs to social media profiles and email lists.

By leveraging audience trust and engagement, affiliates can effectively promote a merchant's product or service, drive traffic, and generate revenue.

Furthermore, affiliate marketing allows marketers to expand their reach without significant upfront costs or investments in traditional advertising channels. Instead, they can leverage affiliates' existing networks and audiences, benefiting from targeted exposure and increased brand visibility. For affiliates, this model provides a flexible and profitable revenue stream. They have the freedom to choose the products or services they advertise based on their audience's interests, expertise, and preferences.

Additionally, affiliates can increase their efforts by diversifying their advertising channels and optimizing their strategies for maximum impact.

Ultimately, affiliate marketing creates a mutually beneficial relationship between the seller and the affiliate, in which both parties benefit from every successful transaction. By leveraging an affiliate's audience, influence, and marketing platform, merchants can expand their customer base and increase sales, while affiliates have the opportunity to monetize their influence and earn passive income.

Profit Potential and Difficulties of Affiliate Marketing

Affiliate marketing offers significant profit potential through passive income streams as affiliates earn commissions for promoting products or services. By leveraging an existing audience or niche, affiliates can access a wide range of products without the need to create products or manage inventory.

However, difficulties include the need to generate consistent traffic, dependence on affiliate program terms and conditions, and the possibility of saturation in competitive markets.

Additionally, maintaining credibility and trust with your audience is important for long-term success, as unethical behavior can harm your reputation and profits.

Let's dig deeper into the profit potential and difficulties of affiliate marketing:

Profit Potential

1. If your advertising channels receive a consistent flow of traffic, affiliate marketing can produce passive income.

2. Because affiliates do not have to spend money on customer service, inventory, or product development, they can reduce their overhead expenses.

3. Affiliates can advertise a broad variety of goods and services in several markets, diversifying their revenue streams and minimizing reliance on a particular good or service.

4. Affiliates don't need to make big financial commitments to enhance their revenue as they expand their audiences and hone their marketing techniques.

5. Affiliates can work from any location and choose their own hours, which is ideal for

anyone seeking more money or geographic independence.

Difficulties

1. Traffic generation: Whether it's your blog, social media accounts, email list, or other promotional avenues, regular traffic is essential to the success of affiliate marketing. It takes ongoing work and optimization to draw in and keep traffic.

2. Program Policy Dependency: Affiliates must abide by the rules established by affiliate programs, which may include payout thresholds, commission rates, and cookie durations. Earnings may directly be impacted by modifications to program policies.

3. Market Saturation: As affiliate marketers vie for the same audience, popular niches may become saturated. Targeted

marketing techniques and distinctive value propositions are necessary to stand out in crowded markets.

4. Credibility and trust: It's critical to keep your audience's trust and credibility. Promoting irrelevant or low-quality products can undermine confidence and harm your brand, which will lower engagement and decrease conversions.

5. Legal and compliance risks: Affiliates are required to abide by rules pertaining to advertising and to openly disclose their affiliate agreements. Penalties, fines, or legal action may follow noncompliance with legal obligations.

All things considered, affiliate marketing presents attractive prospects for flexibility and passive income, but it also presents obstacles that must be solved with commitment, forethought, and moral behavior.

Chapter 2

The Evolution of Affiliate Marketing

The evolution of affiliate marketing traces back to the early days of e-commerce and digital advertising, with its roots firmly planted in the emergence of the internet as a commercial platform. While the concept of affiliate marketing can be traced back to the late 1980s and early 1990s, it wasn't until the mid-to-late 1990s that the model began to take shape and gain traction.

In its nascent stages, affiliate marketing primarily revolved around simple referral programs, where website owners would place banner ads or text links on their sites to promote products or services offered by merchants. These links would include unique tracking codes, allowing merchants to attribute sales or leads generated through these referrals to specific affiliates. Commission structures were often straightforward, with affiliates earning a percentage of the sale or a fixed fee for each referral.

As the internet landscape evolved, so too did affiliate marketing. The late 1990s and early 2000s saw the rise of affiliate networks, which served as intermediaries between merchants and affiliates, facilitating the management of affiliate programs and the tracking of referrals across multiple websites. This development streamlined the affiliate marketing process, making it more accessible to both merchants and affiliates.

The mid-2000s marked a significant turning point for affiliate marketing with the emergence of affiliate marketing platforms and technologies. These platforms provided advanced tracking and reporting capabilities, allowing merchants to optimize their affiliate programs and affiliates to track their performance more effectively. Additionally, the proliferation of content management systems (CMS) and blogging platforms democratized content creation, enabling individuals to build and monetize their online presence through affiliate marketing.

In recent years, affiliate marketing has experienced exponential growth, fueled by the increasing dominance of e-commerce, the rise of social media influencers, and the shift towards performance-based advertising models. Today, affiliate marketing is a multi-billion-dollar industry, with merchants across various industries leveraging affiliate partnerships to drive sales, acquire customers, and expand their reach.

The landscape of affiliate marketing continues to evolve, driven by advancements in technology, changes in consumer behavior, and shifts in digital advertising trends. From its humble beginnings as a simple referral program to its present-day dominance as a cornerstone of digital marketing strategies, the evolution of affiliate marketing reflects the dynamic nature of the online ecosystem and its ongoing adaptation to meet the needs of merchants, affiliates, and consumers alike.

Chapter 3

Choice of Product or Niche

The choice of product is essential to the success of affiliate marketing since it greatly affects the earning potential, audience engagement, and long-term viability of an affiliate. It is impossible to overstate how crucial product selection is since it has an immediate impact on all facets of an affiliate marketer's approach and output.

Here's why choosing the right product is crucial for affiliate marketing:

1. Relevance to Audience: Selecting goods based on the requirements, tastes, and interests of your target audience is very important. You may improve your chances of grabbing your audience's attention, encouraging engagement, and generating conversions by selecting

products that are relevant to them. Knowing the psychographics, demographics, and pain points of your target market is crucial to finding items that cater to their unique requirements and preferences.

2. Credibility and trust: You can increase audience trust and establish your credibility by endorsing reliable, high-quality products. You establish yourself as a reliable resource and raise the possibility of client referrals and returns by recommending goods that live up to expectations. On the other hand, promoting inferior or inappropriate goods might undermine your confidence and harm your reputation, endangering your ability to succeed in affiliate marketing in the long run.

3. Commission Potential: To optimize your profits, it's critical to assess the commission potential of affiliate products.

Although expensive products can result in large profits per sale, low-cost products with a recurring subscription model can eventually produce passive income that is stable. Additionally, you can prioritize products that yield the best marketing returns by assessing how competitive the commission rates are in your business.

4. Market demand and competition: By carrying out comprehensive market research, you can determine which products in your category are most in demand and face the least competition. Through the examination of market trends, consumer behavior, and competition dynamics, it is possible to identify lucrative prospects and leverage underutilized market niches. Furthermore, monitoring rival tactics and merchandise offers insightful information for market positioning and distinctiveness.

5. Quality of Affiliate Programme: Assessing the caliber and dependability of affiliate schemes is crucial for reducing risk and maximizing efficiency. You can select affiliate programs that meet your objectives and expectations by weighing criteria including advertising resources, cookie duration, tracking precision, and payment reliability. Your access to quality goods and customer support services will also be enhanced by collaborating with reliable retailers and affiliate networks, which will enhance your entire affiliate marketing experience.

To put it briefly, the strategic foundation of affiliate marketing is product selection, which determines the affiliate's influence and course of success. Affiliates can position themselves to achieve growth, profitability, and a long-lasting impact on the landscape by placing a high priority on relevance, reliability, commission potential, market demand, and quality of the affiliate program.

Chapter 4

Failing to Build a Solid Foundation

For affiliate marketing to be successful in the long run, a strong foundation must be established. This will provide the framework needed to create strategies that work, cultivate relationships that are beneficial, and experience sustained growth.

Here are the essential actions to laying a strong foundation for affiliate marketing, regardless of your level of experience:

1. Determine your audience and your niche: Determine which market or audience segment best fits your passions, skills, and interests first. To comprehend their demographics, hobbies, and pain issues, do extensive study. By maintaining focus,

you can more effectively customize your content and product recommendations, increasing engagement and conversions.

2. Clearly define your goals and objectives: For your affiliate marketing campaigns, clearly define your measurable goals and objectives. Setting goals will give your actions direction and drive, whether they be for growing your email list, boosting website traffic, or generating targeted cash. Divide your objective into manageable segments and establish due dates so you can monitor your progress and make any necessary revisions.

3. Select top-notch goods and initiatives: To increase your income potential and gain the trust of your audience, use reliable affiliate programs and items. Investigate and assess possible partners using criteria including industry repute, affiliate support, compensation structure, and product quality. Give priority to

collaborating with companies who share your beliefs and provide items that your target market would find useful.

4. Establish a professional online presence: Make the investment to establish a visually appealing, professional online presence that embodies your brand's values and identity. Whether it's your blog, YouTube channel, social media profile, or website, concentrate on offering insightful material that informs, amuses, or resolves user issues. To draw and keep users, optimize your platform for search engines and user experience.

5. Create high-quality content: The foundation of affiliate marketing is content, which is used to generate value, cultivate connections, and increase conversions. Produce interesting, top-notch material that highlights your experience, fulfills the needs of your audience, and truthfully displays affiliate

products. Employ a range of media types, including podcasts, blog articles, videos, and social media postings, to broaden your audience reach and diversify your content approach.

6. Put Relationship Building First: Develop deep connections with your viewers, affiliates, and affiliate managers to promote mutual support, trust, and cooperation. Use social media, emails, and comments to communicate with your audience, establish rapport, and respond to any queries or concerns they may have. Make connections with other affiliates to exchange data, materials, and marketing possibilities that will be advantageous to all parties.

7. Monitor and evaluate performance: Monitor and evaluate your affiliate marketing efforts on a regular basis to pinpoint your campaigns' advantages, disadvantages, and potential areas for

development. Track important indicators such as website traffic, conversion rates, click-through rates, and revenue earned by using analytics software. Refine your approach, maximize the effectiveness of your campaigns, and seize new possibilities using data-driven insights.

You may build a strong foundation for your affiliate marketing activities by adhering to these principles, which will pave the way for success, expansion, and long-term influence in the business world.

Chapter 5

Ignoring Legal and Compliance Issues in Affiliate Marketing

In order to maintain transparency, justice, and moral behavior, affiliates must adhere to a number of laws, rules, and best practices. For this reason, compliance and legal concerns are crucial to affiliate marketing. There are severe repercussions for breaking applicable laws and regulations, including penalties, legal action, and reputational harm.

Affiliates should be aware of the following important legal and compliance issues:

1. FTC Disclosure Mandates: Affiliates are required by the Federal Trade Commission (FTC) to reveal their connections with advertisers and any

payment they get for promoting goods or services. Affiliates must prominently and clearly identify themselves as affiliates in a manner that is simple for customers to comprehend. Any affiliate links or promotional content must be preceded by this disclosure, which cannot be fraudulent or misleading.

2. Data Protection and Privacy Laws: Affiliates are required to abide by rules pertaining to data protection and privacy, such as the California Consumer Privacy Act (CCPA) in the United States and the General Data Protection Regulation (GDPR) in the European Union. This entails getting permission before collecting visitors' personal information, putting data security measures in place, and giving people rights about their personal information.

3. Advertising Standards and Laws: Affiliates are required to abide by the

advertising standards and laws set forth by the appropriate body, such as the National Advertising Division (NAD) in the US or the Advertising Standards Authority (ASA) in the UK. This includes staying away from making untrue or deceptive claims, ensuring advertising is accurate and credible, and staying away from dishonest marketing techniques.

4. Trademarks and Intellectual Property Rights: When endorsing goods or businesses, affiliates are required to uphold trademarks and intellectual property rights. Getting consent to use third-party trademarks, logos, or copyrighted content is part of this, as does preventing intellectual property infringement. Additionally, affiliates must not bid without authorization on branded keywords in paid advertising campaigns.

5. Terms & Conditions of the Affiliate Programme: Affiliates participating in

affiliate programs should read the terms and conditions carefully and abide by them. This includes being aware of the commission schedules, payout limits, cookie durations, and promotional limitations set by affiliate networks or merchants. Program terms violations could lead to the affiliate relationship being terminated and revenues being lost.

6. Endorsement Guidelines: Affiliates are required to abide by the endorsement requirements provided by regulatory bodies, such as the Federal Trade Commission's guidelines in the United States. This entails giving marketers access to relevant connections, offering frank and objective evaluations, and making sure that endorsements fairly represent the affiliate's use of the good or service.

7. Anti-Spam Rules: Affiliates are required to abide by anti-spam rules, which include

the Privacy and Electronic Communications Regulations (PECR) in the United Kingdom and the CAN-SPAM Act in the United States. This entails getting permission before sending marketing emails, offering an opt-out option, and using correct sender information in marketing emails.

Affiliates can conduct themselves in an ethical manner, gain the confidence of their audiences, and reduce the possibility of legal action or responsibility by comprehending and adhering to certain legal and regulatory obligations. Affiliates shall guarantee complete compliance with all applicable rules and regulations in their jurisdiction by consulting with the appropriate authorities or obtaining legal counsel.

Chapter 6

SEO Monitoring and Traffic Generation

An effective affiliate marketing strategy must include SEO monitoring and traffic production in order for affiliates to boost exposure, draw in targeted traffic, and encourage conversions. Affiliates can enhance user experience, boost traffic, and optimize their websites for search engines without having to pay sustainably by employing efficient SEO tactics and monitoring performance metrics.

This is a thorough rundown of affiliate marketing's SEO tracking and traffic generation:

1. Keyword research: Perform comprehensive keyword research to identify relevant search terms that prospective clients might use to locate

goods or services in your industry. To find search volume, competition, and term variations, use keyword research tools. Use commercial long-tail keywords to draw in quality leads and raise conversion rates.

2. Improve on-page SEO: Make sure that the title tags, meta descriptions, headings, and URL structure of your website all correspond to the keywords that are used. Identify and enhance your search engine presence. Ensure that the information in your material is informative, well-structured, and search engine optimized. Avoid keyword stuffing and instead organically include pertinent terms into your writing.

3. Generation and Optimization of Content: Produce top-notch, pertinent content that speaks to your target audience's requirements, inquiries, and interests. Post useful blog entries, product evaluations,

tutorials, or comparison charts that benefit and assist readers. To boost your content's exposure in search results, incorporate rich media features, internal linking, targeted keywords, and schema markup.

4. Link Building: To increase your website's reputation and dependability in the eyes of search engines, build high-quality backlinks from reputable websites and pertinent domains in your industry. Prioritize obtaining backlinks from natural and organic sources by using social media advertising, influencer outreach, content syndication, and guest blogging. Steer clear of link schemes and other black hat SEO techniques that could get you penalized by search engines.

5. Technical SEO Audit: Conduct routine technical SEO audits to find and fix problems that can be affecting how well your website performs in search results. This entails maximizing the crawlability,

internal link structure, crawl speed, and mobile responsiveness of the website. To find and fix problems that can lower your site's visibility and rating, such as broken links, duplicate content, and crawl mistakes, use SEO auditing tools.

6. Analytics & Monitoring for SEO: Track the success of your optimization efforts and pinpoint areas for improvement by keeping an eye on SEO indicators and KPIs. Track metrics like click-through rates, bounce rates, conversion rates, organic traffic, and keyword rankings by utilizing analytics tools such as Google Analytics and Google Search Console. In order to improve your SEO approach and increase outcomes over time, analyze data patterns, user behavior, and search queries.

7. Keep up with SEO trends: To keep your strategy fresh and competitive, stay current with the newest SEO trends,

algorithm changes, and best practices. To stay up to date on new trends, algorithm modifications, and practical advice from SEO specialists, read and subscribe to respectable blogs, forums, and publications in the SEO sector. Try out fresh optimization methods, resources, and approaches to remain on top of trends and enhance your SEO performance over time.

In your affiliate marketing endeavors, you may enhance your website's visibility, draw in quality leads, and raise your conversion rates by giving priority to SEO monitoring and traffic production. Make constant improvements to your SEO approach based on industry trends and data-driven insights to secure long-term success and increase your earning potential as an affiliate marketer.

Chapter 7

Poorly Executed Campaigns and Advertising

Success in affiliate marketing requires an efficient advertising plan. This chapter covers frequent mistakes made by badly done advertisements and campaigns, as well as techniques for coming up with amazing offers that appeal to your target market.

Let's discuss the value of well-run affiliate marketing campaigns and promotions, the dangers of badly run campaigns, methods for developing successful campaigns, how to identify audience needs, and how to stay away from spamming tactics.

The Value of Skillfully Designed Advertisements and Campaigns

1. Reach and visibility: Campaigns and advertisements that are well-run will make affiliate goods and services more visible and accessible, enabling affiliates to engage with a wider audience and draw in new clients.

2. Brand Awareness: Successful marketing initiatives increase brand familiarity and awareness, which bolsters consumer confidence and trust. Affiliates may build a strong brand and message across all initiatives to help them stand out in the marketplace.

3. Engagement and conversions: Strong campaigns connect with their target markets, promote interaction, and increase conversions. Conversion rates can be greatly impacted by persuasive calls to

action, communications, and personalized content.

4. Relationship Development Campaigns that are successful facilitate the development of connections between affiliates and their target audiences, which in turn fosters consumer loyalty. Through delivering value and satisfying the demands of their audiences, affiliates may foster enduring connections and optimize the lifetime value of their customers.

Drawbacks of Badly Done Advertisements and Campaigns

1. Ineffective targeting: Low engagement and wasted advertising budget result from poorly targeted efforts that don't connect with the target demographic. Without a precise grasp of the target audience,

campaigns run the danger of becoming distracted and performing poorly.

2. Deceptive messages: campaigns used ambiguous or inconsistent messaging, which perplexed customers and lessened the brand's message. A brand's credibility can be damaged by inconsistent messaging, which also lessens the impact of advertising.

3. Overbearing or invasive strategies: Bold advertising strategies that irritate and alienate customers, such as pop-ups, auto-playing videos, or excessive retargeting, can damage the brand's reputation. Ad fatigue and decreased engagement can result from intrusive advertising strategies.

4. Inadequate monitoring and measurement: It is challenging to assess campaign efficacy and maximize performance in the absence of adequate monitoring and

measurement. Campaigns that are poorly run may not have obvious KPIs, making it challenging to evaluate their effectiveness or pinpoint areas for development.

Techniques for Developing Successful Campaigns

1. Research on the audience: Investigate your audience in-depth to learn about their demographics, hobbies, habits, and problems. Campaigns should be customized to appeal to target audiences and satisfy their unique requirements.

2. precise objectives and KPIs: Establish precise campaign objectives and KPIs to gauge its effectiveness. Make sure your campaign goals are in line with your overarching business objectives, whether they aim to raise sales, increase website traffic, or increase brand awareness.

3. Creativity and persuasive messaging: To draw in viewers, arouse feelings, and clearly convey a value proposition, create persuasive content and messaging. In order to captivate your audience and inspire action, use persuading language, captivating imagery, and storytelling approaches.

4. Omnichannel strategy: Utilize a variety of platforms and channels to reach a wide range of people and increase visibility. To increase the reach and impact of your campaign, combine paid advertising, social media, email marketing, content marketing, and influencer partnerships.

How to Recognise the Demands of Your Audience and Steer Clear of Spam Tactics

1. Empathy mapping and sympathy: To comprehend the needs, motives, and pain points of the audience, engage in empathy exercises and empathy mapping. Create advertisements that tackle practical issues and provide solutions that appeal to the target audience.

2. Permission-based marketing: Give priority to permission-based campaigns that honor the privacy and choices of customers. Prior to sending promotional communications or gathering users' personal information, get their express consent.

3. Customisation and Pertinence: Adapt material to each audience segment's interests and preferences in a personalized manner. Steer clear of impersonal and spammy communications that are general and one-size-fits-all.

4. Openness and disclosure: Be open and truthful about your affiliate connections and your goals for advertising. To uphold credibility and trust with your audience, be sure to declare any sponsored material, affiliate relationships, or paid endorsements in full.

Affiliates may develop successful advertising campaigns and initiatives that connect with their audiences, encourage engagement and conversion, and build enduring relationships with customers by putting these tactics into practice and avoiding typical errors.

Chapter 8

Neglecting to Develop Relationships

In affiliate marketing, relationship building is crucial for several reasons:

1. Credibility and Trust: Developing Relationships with Your Audience Promotes Credibility and Trust. By continuously offering insightful articles, suggestions, and fixes for their issues, you position yourself as a reliable authority in your industry. Building trust is essential for retaining long-term client loyalty and increasing conversions.

2. Recurring sales and recommendations: Strong bonds encourage referrals and repeat sales. Satisfied clients who rely on your advice are more likely to make

repeat purchases and refer others to your goods or services. Positive word-of-mouth recommendations from contented clients are extremely valuable and can greatly boost your reputation and sales.

3. Differentiation and competitive advantage: In a cutthroat industry, solid connections help you stand out from the competition. Consumers are more inclined to select brands with which they identify and feel valued. Developing a genuine connection with your audience helps you differentiate yourself from competitors that only focus on transactions.

4. Thoughts and criticism: Connect offers insightful analysis and comments from your viewers. By interacting with your audience, you can gain a deeper understanding of their requirements, passions, and problems. Your product offers, content production, and marketing methods can all benefit from this input,

which will enable you to better focus your efforts on your target market.

5. Possibilities for Collaboration: Developing connections with influencers, affiliates, and other business leaders creates chances for cooperation. Joint ventures, co-promotions, and affiliate relationships are examples of collaborative initiatives that can broaden your audience, introduce you to new ones, and benefit all parties.

6. Extended success: The cornerstone of long-term success in affiliate marketing is relationships. While speedy transactions could result in profits in the near term, building deep relationships with your audience will eventually lead to profitable and sustainable growth. Building relationships will pay off in the form of devoted clients, repeat business, and favorable word of mouth.

Developing relationships in affiliate marketing is crucial for fostering cooperation, gaining insightful knowledge, developing trust, and achieving long-term success. Prioritizing relationship-building helps affiliates stand out from the competition, develop a devoted following, and prosper in the cutthroat world of affiliate marketing. Building relationships with your audience and affiliate partners is crucial to affiliate marketing because it promotes loyalty, trust, and credibility.

Affiliates can effectively cultivate relationships in the following ways:

1. Authenticity and Transparency: In your communications with affiliate partners and your audience, act with transparency and authenticity. Establish credibility by being open about your affiliate connections and the reasons behind your product or service promotion. Openness fosters trust and establishes the

groundwork for enduring partnerships built on honesty, respect, and reciprocity.

2. Deliver value: Put your attention towards giving your audience something of value through insightful analysis, practical advice, and top-notch material. Attend to their wants, resolve their issues, and give them pertinent knowledge that improves their experiences or enriches their life. By continuously offering value, you build audience loyalty and establish yourself as a reliable resource.

3. Participate and exchange words: Communicate with your audience frequently via a range of platforms, such as social media, email newsletters, blog comments, and discussion boards. Pay attention to what they have to say, fulfill their demands, and have deep interactions with them. By encouraging two-way contact, you build rapport, acquire data,

and show that you are dedicated to fulfilling the demands of your audience.

4. Foster Community: By bringing like-minded individuals together and encouraging deep connections, you may build a feeling of community around your brand or specialty. Encourage audience members to collaborate, participate, and share expertise. By establishing connections and offering a forum for community involvement, you'll strengthen bonds and build a devoted following.

5. Collaboration with Affiliate Partners: Cultivate a rapport with affiliate partners through cooperation, communication, and respect. To achieve shared success, set clear expectations, be transparent about goals and objectives, and collaborate. Create a nurturing atmosphere where both sides can develop and gain from working together.

6. Provide assistance and backing: Take the initiative to assist and support your affiliate partners and audience. Provide counsel, respond to inquiries, and offer ideas for overcoming their difficulties. By being eager to assist and encourage people, you forge stronger bonds with them and establish yourself as a useful ally.

7. Remain genuine and consistent: Remain genuine and consistent in all of your communications, interactions, and brand. Throughout your affiliate marketing endeavors, stay loyal to your principles, convictions, and distinctive voice. Maintaining consistency in your brand identity and building trust will help you stand out in a crowded market and establish stronger bonds with your audience.

Affiliates can sustain enduring relationships with their audiences and affiliate partners by giving priority to relationship-building initiatives in affiliate marketing. Through prioritizing authenticity, value, engagement, collaboration, and support, affiliates may establish a robust community, cultivate loyalty, and achieve sustained success in their affiliate marketing activities.

Chapter 9

Lack of Tracking and Analytics

In affiliate marketing, tracking and analytics are essential tools that enable affiliates to assess, evaluate, and enhance their campaigns for optimal effectiveness and financial gain.

This is a thorough explanation of affiliate marketing tracking and analytics:

1. Monitor performance indicators:

- Affiliates keep an eye on things using technology and tracking techniques to monitor various performance indicators, such as website traffic, click-through rate (CTR), conversion rates, prices, and sales and revenue from affiliate links.

- Tracking tools such as third-party tracking software, affiliate network dashboards, and Google Analytics offer insightful data on audience behavior, campaign performance, and roadmaps.

2. models of attribution:
- Attribution models assign credit to various touchpoints in the customer journey, linking particular marketing channels or interactions to conversions.

- The last click, initial click, linear, and multi-touch attribution models are popular attribution models in affiliate marketing; they all provide data. Particular information regarding how affiliate channels affect conversions.

3. Monitoring Conversions:
- Affiliates may assess how well their advertising campaigns are resulting in desired activities, like sales, by using conversion monitoring.

- Affiliates utilize conversion tracking codes, or pixels, on their websites to monitor user activity and link conversions to the appropriate affiliate campaigns or channels.

4. Analytics of Performance:
    - Affiliates can use analytics tools to examine performance data, spot patterns, and assess how various marketing tactics affect key performance indicators.

    - Affiliates may assess the efficacy of campaigns, optimize them for better outcomes, and allocate resources to certain channels or campaigns by tracking performance data over time.

5. Optimization and A/B testing:
    - Comparing variants of marketing content, such as advertisements, landing pages, or email subject lines that encourage conversions, is known as A/B testing.

- Affiliates employ analytics to carry out A/B testing, assess the effects of modifications, and enhance campaigns by utilizing the knowledge acquired from testing.

6. Segmenting the Audience:
    - Affiliates can use analytics tools to divide their audiences into groups according to demographics, behavior, or other characteristics in order to better understand the needs and interests of.

    - Affiliates may increase relevance and engagement by customizing offers, content, and marketing messaging to target specific audience segments through audience segmentation.

7. Performance Reporting:
    - Affiliates generate performance reports for customers, affiliate managers, and themselves using tracking data and analytics.

- Performance reporting offers insights into affiliate partnership effectiveness, ROI, and campaign performance, assisting stakeholders in decision-making and marketing strategy optimization.

8. Compliance and Fraud Detection:
    - Tracking and analytics technologies assist affiliates in keeping an eye on adherence to the requirements of the affiliate program and spotting fraudulent conduct, such as click fraud or affiliate link hijacking.

    - Through the detection of questionable trends or deviations in data monitoring, branches can proactively address risks and safeguard their earnings and standing.

Overall, monitoring and analytics are essential to the success of affiliate marketing because they give affiliates the data-driven insights they need to maximize campaigns, encourage conversions, and meet their business objectives. Affiliates may maximize return on investment, make well-informed decisions, and maintain an advantage in the highly competitive affiliate marketing space by skillfully utilizing tracking technologies and analytics tools.

Chapter 10

People Harmed By Dubious Affiliate Schemes

Not all affiliate marketing programmes are made equal in the huge world of affiliate marketing. The dangers connected with dubious affiliate programmes, how to spot trustworthy affiliate programmes, warning signs to look out for, and methods to safeguard your reputation and brand integrity are all covered in detail below:

Dangers Connected with Dubious Affiliate Schemes

1. Late or nonpayment of commission: Certain dubious affiliate programs might not give affiliates credit for their referrals or might put payments on hold

indefinitely, which would frustrate and cost affiliates money.

2. Low-quality goods or services: If the product is of low quality, associations with programs that provide such goods or services could harm your credibility and reputation with your audience.

3. Dishonest or unlawful actions: Affiliate networks that use dishonest or unlawful practices, such as spamming, deceptive advertising, or phishing, run the danger of breaking the law and damaging your company's reputation.

4. Fraudulent Activities and Stuffing Cookies: Affiliates that commit click fraud, cookie stuffing, or other dishonest acts may jeopardize your affiliate commissions and harm your connections to affiliate networks and suppliers.

How To Determine Trustworthy Affiliate Networks

1. Examine the seller's track record: Before enrolling in their program, properly investigate both the seller and the affiliate network. Check for endorsements, comments, and reviews from other affiliates to determine their credibility.

2. Consider the product's quality: Analyze the suitability and quality of the good or service that the affiliate program offers. Select shows that have reliable, high-quality products that meet the audience's wants and interests.

3. Examine the commission schedule: Examine the length of the cookie, payment conditions, and commission structure for your affiliate program. To optimize your earning potential, search for programs that provide suitable cookie

lengths, fair and competitive commissions, and timely payments.

4. Examine the terms of the affiliate agreement: Examine and study the Affiliate Agreement or Program's Terms of Service with great attention. To make sure they are in line with your company's objectives and core values, pay close attention to the terms of payment, promotional limitations, and compliance requirements.

Warning Signs to be Aware of in Affiliate Marketing

1. Impractical assurances: Affiliate programs that provide implausible guarantees of success or income immediately should be avoided. Sincere affiliate programs place a strong emphasis on diligence, commitment, and reasonable expectations.

2. Lack of Transparency: Steer clear of programs that are opaque or that give ambiguous information on their commission plans, goods, or conditions of payment. Building trust and ensuring a mutually successful alliance require transparency.

3. Ineffective Communication: When an affiliate program responds poorly to inquiries, provides evasive responses, or takes a long time to address complaints, it may indicate a lack of professionalism or other issues.

4. Bad Reviews or Complaints: Pay heed to any bad feedback on the functionality, dependability, or performance of the Chapter submitted by affiliates or other industry experts.

How to Keep Your Brand Integrity and Reputation Intact

1. Comply with your principles: Select affiliate networks that fit your morals, beliefs, and brand image. Encourage your audience to use goods or services that you firmly believe in and endorse.

2. Reveal affiliate connections: Always be upfront and honest with your readers about any affiliate ties you may have. Transparent disclosure fosters integrity and generates confidence with your audience, which helps you stay credible.

3. Monitor the effectiveness of your campaign: Keep an eye on important indicators and the effectiveness of your affiliate marketing to make sure they are meeting your expectations and goals. Be ready to make changes or sever ties with

underperforming or troublesome programs.

4. Keep yourself informed and current: Keep up on developments in affiliate marketing regulations, industry trends, and best practices. To safeguard oneself against potential dangers and liabilities, educate yourself on typical mistakes, legal requirements, and ethical values.

5. Report suspected fraud or unethical behavior: Contact the relevant authorities, such as affiliate networks or regulatory organizations, if you come across questionable activity or unethical behavior in an affiliate program. By disclosing wrongdoing, the affiliate marketing ecosystem's accountability and integrity are preserved.

In the highly competitive world of affiliate marketing, affiliates can reduce risk, safeguard their reputation, and preserve the integrity of their brands by being watchful, picky, and proactive when selecting affiliate programs.

Chapter 11

Prevent Burnout and Foster Long-Term Success

The most successful individuals recognise the need of guarding against burnout, practicing balancing techniques, and developing a mindset that supports long-term affiliate marketing success and fulfillment.

Managing Expectations in Affiliate Marketing

Setting reasonable goals and being aware of the realities of the industry are key to managing expectations in affiliate marketing.

This is how to accomplish it successfully:

1. Educate Yourself: Learn everything you can about affiliate marketing before you start. Recognise how it operates, the possible income, and the time and effort needed to be successful.

2. Make sensible goals: Based on your abilities, resources, and industry trends, define your goals. Aim for gradual growth rather than instant success.

3. Put Quality Above Quantity: Give your audience's needs more importance than counting how many affiliate links or advertisements you post. Higher conversion rates are the result of authentic recommendations and high-quality content.

4. Know the Sales Funnel: Acknowledge that not all clicks will lead to a transaction. Recognise the normal conversion rates in your niche and the sales funnel. You can control your

expectations and stay out of frustration by doing this.

5. Monitor and Modify: Keep a close eye on your performance and modify your tactics as necessary. Examine the strategies that are and are not working, and be prepared to adjust your approach to the market as circumstances change.

6. Exercise Patience: Just as Rome wasn't built in a day, an affiliate marketing business can't be successful overnight. Recognise that regular effort and dedication will provide benefits, so be patient and persistent.

7. Communicate with Partners: Keep lines of communication open when working with affiliate networks or specific retailers. Recognise their policies and expectations to guarantee a win-win collaboration.

8. Diversify Your Sources of money: You shouldn't rely completely on affiliate marketing. Spread out your sources of income to reduce risks and maintain a steady income.

You can position yourself for long-term success in the affiliate marketing business by controlling your expectations and adopting a realistic approach.

Avoiding Burnouts and Maintaining Balance

In affiliate marketing, staying balanced and avoiding burnout are critical to long-term productivity and wellbeing. This is how you do it:

1. Set Boundaries: Clearly define the boundaries between your personal and

professional lives. Set aside specified times for work and adhere to them. Avoid the urge to work excessively on weekends or late into the night.

2. Take Regular Breaks: Throughout your workday, schedule regular pauses for rest and rejuvenation. Taking occasional breaks from work, be it a quick stroll, meditation session, or coffee break, might help reduce burnout and enhance focus.

3. Prioritize Self-Care: Taking good care of your physical and emotional well-being is an important part of self-care. A healthy diet, regular exercise, adequate sleep, and stress-relieving hobbies like yoga or mindfulness meditation are all important.

4. Delegate and Outsource: Admit that you are not capable of handling every task on your own. To free up time and energy, assign duties that can be completed by others or think about outsourcing key

parts of your firm, such as administrative or content creation.

5. Set Realistic Expectations: Refrain from overcommitting by establishing reasonable expectations and goals. Divide more complex undertakings into smaller, more doable ones, and concentrate on finishing each one gradually.

6. Learn to Say No: Exercise discretion in the opportunities and tasks you accept. Recognise when to say no to collaborations or assignments that could be too much for you or that don't fit with your values or aims.

7. Remain Organised: Use tools like task lists, calendars, or project management software to stay on top of your assignments, due dates, and obligations. Reducing stress and avoiding overwhelm can be achieved by maintaining organization.

8. Remain Informed: Avoid isolating yourself. Maintain relationships with loved ones, coworkers, and industry peers. Embrace a network of people who are there to support you and who can provide you insight, counsel, and encouragement.

9. Keep an Eye on Your Mental Health: If you find yourself experiencing overwhelm, tension, or anxiety, get treatment. If you need help, don't be afraid to get in touch with a licensed counselor or therapist.

10. Celebrate Your Success: Regardless of how tiny, give yourself a moment to recognise and appreciate your accomplishments. Acknowledging your development and successes can inspire and uplift you.

You can prioritize your well-being while avoiding burnout, maintaining balance, and sustaining long-term success in affiliate marketing by putting these principles into practice.

Long-Term Plans for Sustainable Success

Adopting long-term growth and stability-promoting tactics is necessary for affiliate marketing success.

The following are important long-term tactics to think about:

1. Create a Strong Brand: Make an investment to create a brand that appeals to your target market. Prioritize producing insightful material, building relationships, and becoming recognised as an authority in your field.

2. Pay Attention to High-Quality Content: In affiliate marketing, content is king. Provide valuable, interesting, and educational information to your audience that is of the highest caliber. Continually create material for blogs, social media, videos, podcasts, and other platforms.

3. Diversify Your Sources of Traffic: It can be dangerous to rely just on one source of traffic. Use a variety of avenues to diversify your traffic, including paid advertising, social media, email marketing, and organic search. This lessens reliance on any one platform and lessens the effects of algorithmic modifications or oscillations.

4. Create an Email List: One of the best strategies for nurturing leads and boosting sales is still email marketing. Create an email list of interested subscribers, then stay in touch with them on a regular basis

by sending them recommendations, promotions, and tailored content.

5. Optimize for SEO: To increase your website's exposure and organic traffic, spend money on search engine optimization (SEO). Research the best keywords to utilize, make your content and website structure better, and concentrate on giving them a seamless experience.

6. Remain Current and Adjust: The affiliate marketing environment is ever-changing. Keep abreast on developing technology, algorithmic updates, and industry trends. To stay on top of things, be adaptable and willing to change your tactics.

7. Build Relationships: Develop enduring bonds with affiliate managers, other affiliates, and your audience. Communicate with your readers via email, forums, and social media. Work together

with other affiliates to share opportunities and ideas.

8. Put an emphasis on Long-Term Value: Give long-term value creation for your audience top priority rather than pursuing quick profits. Pay close attention to meeting their requirements, finding solutions to their issues, and providing outstanding experiences that will entice them to return.

You will be in a better position to develop a successful business over time and attain long-term success in affiliate marketing if you put these long-term tactics into practice.

Conclusion

In conclusion, "Affiliate Marketing for Beginners: The Definitive Guide to Overcoming the Deadly Mistakes of Affiliate Marketing" serves as a valuable resource for affiliate marketers navigating the intricate world of affiliate marketing.

By highlighting the potential hazards, traps, and alerts associated with dubious actions, this manual empowers affiliates to make informed decisions, mitigate risks, safeguard their reputations, and uphold the integrity of their brands.

In today's dynamic affiliate marketing environment, affiliates can avoid costly mistakes and cultivate a profitable and lasting business by implementing ethical marketing strategies, understanding audience needs, and selecting reliable affiliate programs.

By prioritizing honesty, authenticity, and value creation in their interactions with audiences, affiliate partners, and industry colleagues, affiliate marketers can establish enduring success and influence in the competitive landscape of affiliate marketing.

www.ingramcontent.com/pod-product-compliance
Lightning Source LLC
Chambersburg PA
CBHW070350230526
45471CB00006B/2509